# IS IT
## CALLED
## REVERSE
# *RACISM*?

SHARIF NSUBUGA

## DEDICATION

Our lives may seemingly never matter to you. We're born invisible, ready to fit both world's stereotypes, but still suffering in silence, and forgotten every day. We grow up confused since our body features do not only belong to a single race.

Denied a right to belong due to our whiteness and discriminated against. Our voices became silenced, "We should shut our mouths" whenever we tried to be heard. Is there a privilege of belonging to a single certain box?

And if so, we never chose to be born this way. How could I change who I am? This came as our heritage, however, the unequal personal treatment we get subjected to trodden me down.

I can be your daughter, and I personally don't believe in race classification, but why have I been institutionalized into racial hierarchies? I never invaded or led to any systemic inequality. I am a symbol of togetherness because my parents chose to "love" and never saw color.

Sharif Nsubuga, the author of Cosmopolitan picked inspiration from the events that happened to "The South African colored community," Individuals who were not either black or white that faced tons of discrimination and they were seen as a residual group. Separated in every area of life, and even lost their right to vote in the 1956s.

# CONTENTS

# SELF-ACCEPTANCE

I am a biracial woman, married to a white man, and we have three children. My eldest has brown eyes, black hair, and darker features, whereas his two younger siblings have blue hazel eyes and lighter skin than him.

I never allowed my son to introduce himself as black or white, on forms, I've always marked both races, and I explained to him that being a mixed race came as our heritage.

And if he claimed he belonged to only one race, he would be denying himself and the parent of that race. Back then, eighteen years or more, there used to be no books or shows with mixed-race children.

His father and I encouraged them,

to embrace their mixed race, in a world, less accepting.

I have white skin and am legitimately a Native American, nearly every race has "white" and "black" skin people, well known as the coloreds. Most of us had no idea about our family history, I didn't want my sons to feel lost.

Yes, my eldest son got bullied in school, for identifying as mixed many times. He got told he's nothing else, but black and he should get used to it.

White people will only see him as black, and they will treat him accordingly.

"But that isn't my experience at all." He addressed a medium-sized dark-skinned gentleman, with afro hair in a large classroom.

"Why do you hate your blackness?"

The chubby chocolate-colored girl came up as well, trying to kill my son's confidence.

"The 1drop rule says you're black, whether you accept it or not," Eugene assured him.

Regardless of the sketchy outdated law, my husband and I never allowed anyone to define our son's origin.

This country has become so obsessed with race; would you imagine a young child being bullied in school for identifying with all he is?

"You're just light-skinned." The chubby girl never allowed him to respond.

"It has nothing to do with skin color." He suddenly spoke.

"Logic would!" Eugene, a much older boy, threw shade at my son.

"Phenotypically I have beautiful

African features, but the fact is, I'm not black."

"I see Black, my dude." They began laughing at him while walking out of the classroom.

1

Could I call this reverse racism? But I don't believe in such, we are all humans. Therefore, we all have the propensity to be racists. I grew up in a neighborhood that had ninety-nine percentage of white people, but I only experienced racism from the black people, those I thought knew how we walked in the same shoes.

I loved my son's guts, he talked his truth, the exact way we had raised him, bold and kind, and he had goodness within him. Never spread hate, he just protected his father's side as well.

I couldn't imagine how hurtful it could make their white father when his children only acknowledged their blackness, completely ignoring his white side. That would be horrible, and I would never let my boys do that to him.

I am a biracial woman. I didn't walk around with a banner declaring I had a black mother, but I dealt with racism at every level from black people.

I never wanted to use my black percentage as a defense mechanism, "Ooh, no, you've got it wrong, I'm half black," I wholly embraced my American and Nigerian heritage.

I never used my whiteness as some badge of honor, or did I use my blackness as a victim bludgeon.

My mother, may her soul rest in peace, never got offended by this nor did she ever feel ignored. I simply acknowledged both races, because that's who I am.

My biracial sons knew how the world looked at them, but they never denied their white side. To do so, they would have denied their father, his parents, and relatives. Every other white person had a hand in raising them.

As a daughter of a foreign mother, my mom sent my brother and me to her country for months, to learn her culture. Honestly, she never had the time and patience to teach us, she had a lot of anger issues, and she had many physical blows with my father.

I wondered how they crossed paths because they hated each other, but they had to raise us.

In the evenings, her Jamaican friend and she used to hang around, so she took both of us, to Auntie Ladonya's place. However, they both used to sit around her broad front compound, smoking some maulana, and enjoying their day.

Without her supervision, we wandered around, until she realized my dad could be returning home from his work. She then panicked, and drove insanely fast, totally out of her mind.

# 2

Endangering our lives, her eyes became reddish, due to the smoke, but she drove her lower-boxed car.

But still, this didn't capture me until they took us for our pool day, at the town's main swimming pool. In a long course, one hundred and sixty-four feet in length, they sat on a sunlounger, chair-like placed at the swimming pool deck.

As we played in the pool together, a middle-aged white gentleman came with his six-year-old child. He desperately wanted his son to play with us, so as a responsible parent, he approached my mother and her Jamaican friend.

"Good afternoon, ma'am, how's

your day?" He interrupted their chat.

"Yes, what?" Her friend addressed him, he looked confused, he had no idea who could've been our mother.

"Okay, may my son play with yours in the pool?"

Her face looked at us, we wanted to play with him. My brother seemed to be the more excited one since they were of the same age group. We stood still, making begging faces for her.

"Hmm, you can…"

"Are you being serious?" Her friend interrupted her.

"No, they can't." She continued for her.

The gentleman remained bothered wondering what he had done, you see, he became overwhelmed, having many thoughts running through his mind about the issue. These were kids, playing around, and could harm no one.

"Why?" He suddenly asked, drawing their attention again.

It became ridiculous for her since she judged him based on his color, she had no logic in the matter. Racism rang the bell here, it never mattered in this country, because she perpetuated it.

"I am forty-three years old, my whole life I have treated people with respect and love. But these past five years…" Everyone around could feel the tension, he had so much love to give, "I've experienced more hatred coming from a few black people than I have ever seen, now it's my son."

Uncontrollable teardrops rolled out of his hazel eyes, and my mother stood up, buried in so much guilt.

"We're sorry, man."

"I am not, not in front of the colonizer."

# 3

"Not every white person came from the plantation owners or lived in the States. A lot of white people died to free the slaves in this country."

"Here we go again, playing the victim card."

"Landoya?" My mom wondered.

"What? He appears to be dealing with lots of swing moods and emotions. That's the exact reason a racist person could give."

"I predicted nearly the same energy with you, it does beckon the question within me." He used a serious tone, "Between you and me, who is worse? The monster or the people that let the monster loose."

"Yeah, that's why I am moving my

family from yours now, you are damn crazy man." She raised her voice on him, her palms sparkled fire as if she wanted to throw some jabs at him.

I could see him, scared for his life. He walked backward, away from her. His six-year-old little son just wanted to play with us, no color needed to be involved, very sad, indeed. Hatred brought pain to the world, regardless of whomever it came from.

"I pray for people toting hatred within their hearts to make them sick and old." He cursed while walking away from the scene with his son.

Maybe she hated the fact, that our mother's offspring completely dismissed her race, and Auntie Landoya found us disgusting.

I am of mixed ethnicity, and I've loved every part of it, having a diverse background and heritage.

And whenever I met fellow mixed students at school insisting, they were black, it sounded so illogical and sad that they had an obvious identity crisis.

Genetics must be an amazing thing, and denying any part of our heritage could be a disgrace and dishonor to those who fought to get us here.

I noticed both sides, "black and white" treating us differently, we go through an identity crisis because we could never be white enough for the white side or black enough for the black side.

I remember being addressed by my mother's relatives as a "Mzungu" when I paid my first visit to Lagos. They spoke in their language, but in English with me, regardless of my effort to learn to speak Yoruba.

Our identity limited how much our mother's relatives were willing to share about their culture. In fact, our cousins had more privileges to learn about the rich Nigerian culture than we did.

In high school, whenever they asked where my brother and I came from, I said both, the States and Nigeria. However, my mother's relatives claimed in their culture we only belonged to our father's side.

They never trusted us; I could tell the tension whenever I sat down with them. Our cousins and we used to get along, we never saw color, at the age of seven years old.

We used to play and run after one another in the soiled playgrounds, but later, my uncles might have told them something, they distanced and divided up our friendship based on certain differences.

On an unfortunate morning, my brother and I came out with a ball to join our cousins, Adaeze, Chibuike, Abosede, and Afamefuna who had already begun running around.

"The light bright, and mixed black king and queen." Abosede began talking, drawing everyone's attention, you see, we were never taught to see color until our uncles started talking about it.

"You don't appear ambiguous, you're just white!" Chibuike continued.

By then, a rumor used to spread that we didn't belong to their family, they talked that we might have been stolen from the hospital, maybe changed mistakenly because we never shown any black genes on our physical features.

"Why is it anyone's business? It's becoming too personal." I tried to kill the unnecessary tension.

"I see a strong individual, and I think it's cool to have hazel eyes."

Afamefuna, one of my uncle's daughters addressed us while smiling, she had desires of becoming the second Nigerian president who was a woman. She never saw color, nor cared about how we looked.

"Yes, be aware queen," She whispered to me, "It's okay to identify as mixed. Things shouldn't always be black and white."

"I'm confused, lol. Are you white or descended from our black auntie but came out pale?" Adaeze, the eldest, couldn't let it slide, he wanted to confirm the rumor I told you about.

"Frankly, people are just people. You're supposed to see only good."

"But I only see white, come on,

Afamefuna, just look at them."

My little brother's ball suddenly fell off his tiny palms as he began crying loudly. The division hit both of us that day, I wanted to be there for us. I had no idea how the race thing worked until I hit my teenage era.

# 5

People in the States must be obsessed with race, what could be wrong with being the best of both worlds? In college, my friend Cynthia Lennon used to identify as black. However, both of her parents were Native Americans, her mixed father must have had a single drop of black blood because he looked white totally.

The 1drop rule never existed in other states. In the United Kingdom, that concept doesn't exist, if you are born by both races, you identify as black mixed because that's who you are.

When I think about myself, "what I identify as" the last thing that may even come to my mind could be anything to do with race.

Not in any particular order, but I

would think of myself, my adorable sons, and my husband.

A man who valued hard work, someone with a strong sense of integrity, a highly flawed, and imperfect individual I greatly love.

He kept on thriving to do better, even when I introduced him to my mother's family. Regardless of visible rejection, he never reacted or lost his cool.

These people never welcomed us and during the introduction of my husband in Ikotun, Nigeria, they talked about my sons. Still in doubt about the heritage of my sons and me.

We were no longer young, imagine what could now come out of their mouths. Some had successful careers like Adaeze, who owned a milk production company in Lagos, and

Chibuike became a well-known TV personality, unfortunately, Afamefuna ended up a joke, she had a failed career.

When her father, my uncle, died, none of our uncles helped to raise her fees, she ended up dropping out from the University of Lagos, in her second year of bachelor's in law.

Yes, she still had her dream to become the second female president of Nigeria.

"Well, I didn't see this coming, I last saw you in 2016, and now you're a married woman." She spoke.

"It's really unfortunate about my uncle," I tried to console her.

"Thank you."

"It's angering like how disgusting American people can be." I heard whispers, they talked about my eldest son, his black heritage was visibly noticed, but now, they spread a rumor about how I slept with other men, specifically, African American men to give birth to him.

I must have had an affair to give birth to a son with African features, I quickly grabbed, a glass of wine, and I took it quickly, as I noticed everyone's eyes on my son.

"That is a manipulative statement, totally blown out of proportion, and a play of words. If you look at him, you'll realize they resemble their father." I addressed the elderly woman who had a lot to say about my son.

"Say the truth child." Her ghostly face folded as she addressed me.

"I am not your child." I didn't know this woman, but in the African setting, our mothers could call out their old friends to show off during these ceremonies.

At that moment, my cousin, Adaeze

whispered I sounded ridiculous, and hysterical because I couldn't stop arguing with an elderly. In the African culture, the elderly could never be wrong, so they respected them the most.

But it could be an abuse of respect, especially when the world has been given to you, and all you had to do was encourage, protect, and cherish the younger generation rather than tear it down.

"Ha-ha thank you for coming ma, your spoken beautiful words are more meaningful, of course, they come from an intelligent person."

Abosede tried to calm the energy that had become tense between the elderly woman and me. He had taken over the home responsibilities for our dead uncle since women never inherited in the Yoruba culture.

The only person who greatly loved me, even outdoors, so yeah, I would rather think about my husband than race. It could be the time for us, people, to stop thinking of ourselves in terms of race.

It's not a thing we have control over, so I don't know why we put it so high up on the list of things we identify with. I could identify with far more good positive things about me such as achievements, no one has ever achieved, "their race."

They were born into it regardless of any contribution of their own, so why do we put so much emphasis on it? Why do we have to identify with either race? I could identify with my name.

Arguing with a Hispanic woman in

Atlanta, that whites do experience racism as well, in a massive coffee shop.

"You're white." She addressed me, trying to play the victim card. Yes, I looked white, but I had a dark-skinned Nigerian mother.

# 7

I am told my white skin meant I have to mark white on all forms, even when I am mixed, so if perhaps I had a darker white skin, I could mark others on the forms.

Well, I experienced racist remarks because of my white skin, by simply offering to let three people in front of me in the coffee line. They had less than five items they wanted to buy, yet I had many, that's why I offered to let them buy first.

Two Hispanic women, and an elderly dark-skinned man, the younger lady with the elder black man accused me of only being nice because I felt guilty for my white ancestors' doings.

"Being antiracism is being antiwhite, doesn't that mean they're telling on themselves? Acknowledging they're racists?" When I told her I am mixed, she addressed the elderly man while laughing at me.

It felt like they pulled these vague terms out of the bible.

"I am mixed, but sick of the white people's stories of being racists because most of them are not," I spoke, drawing their attention.

The Hispanic women's mouths opened involuntarily; they never expected my response.

"Beach flamingos, you were correct then, and you are correct now. You're always right. We are to understand you, as usual." The elderly man assured me.

Yes, I didn't get surprised, that had become my lifestyle, being judged by my skin color, in Nigeria, they think I am rich, every time I traveled there without my mother.

So, when I am nice, I'm a racist? In fact, the Hispanic women then thought I was Hispanic. That could be a valid reason why I also let their dark-skinned grandpa pass me, trying not to show that I only favored my people.

I explained I wasn't Hispanic, and then she automatically assumed I was white, who felt guilty for what "my people did to hers!"

"Nope, I am not white either…" Their grandpa cut me off and began to firmly address his granddaughters.

"You need to be quiet, your ancestors were sold by their own people, and stop acting like you know anything about struggles." His angry tone raised, creating the uncontrolled tense environment, "Take your ass outside after apologizing to all of these ladies for acting like a fool in here."

I couldn't believe it. My tiny body shook in disbelief, how could someone be so judgmental like that elderly man?

8That man referred to me as white, deep down I'm sure he knew I am mixed. Then I realized it never mattered what people wanted you to identify with, this world had bigger problems than a mixed person who never wanted to acknowledge she had white blood too.

Not every biracial person should claim to be black, I constantly get called Hispanic because I am completely white, with no dark-skinned features, and I have always wondered why most mixed people claim to be black.

Why can't we just acknowledge both races? There must be no reverse racism.

Whites hating blacks or anyone else based on skin color or ethnicity must be racists, and Blacks hating whites or anyone else based on skin color or ethnicity must be racists as well. There should be double standards for accountability.

Apart from my mother, I was raised by a white family, in a white town that only had a few black people. That must be a valid reason why my mother drove those many miles to see her friend, Auntie Landoya.

I am on the lighter side, with little thin curly hair, so yeah, I definitely could pass for being white. However, I experienced slight racism from school peers as a kid, and as a kid it never became serious.

I grew up trying to understand how I could blend in with both races, but the black students never tried to welcome me, I dealt with racism from them regardless of other hateful incidents they talked about.

"What kind of a black person she is? I don't understand... pretty though!" These were some of the terrible remarks they made.

"Unreal right like where the duck does she come from." The chubby chocolate-skinned girl assured the bunch of black girls.

"But she just looks like us." One of the girls tried to defend me.

"Exactly, that is what racism is, we

should quit talking about her color. We're all humans, not a color." An older male student came into their conversation. He had stood opposite them and knew exactly who they discussed.

"I just see a good-looking girl; I don't care if she's white or black." He continued.

9 You see, the black students labeled me as white, they subjected me to every form of racism, which made me feel isolated from identifying with their side, but it was my birthright. As a mixed person, I looked stupid to deny myself.

I've always acknowledged both sides, but the second I'm proud of who I am, the black people rushed to tell me how wrong I am to be happy with being black and white.

So yeah, I could never refer to being

a person of color without black people screaming at me for claiming my black side since my skin is lighter, yet I can never acknowledge my white side either without them screaming that I am a racist for not referring to my black side.

It destroyed them, you could see envy in their eyes, one step before screaming at me. Funny how that worked for them, none of it made sense, just leave me alone. I am proud of being mixed, please stop projecting your insecurities on me. Black privilege must be so real!

I couldn't insult any of my parent's heritage, and denying one of them could cause a total lack of respect. I am a biracial woman, and I am sticking to it, even though my mother's family ridiculed me for talking like a white, they denied me right from the start.

I hate I didn't have a proper opportunity to learn and cherish my black side like my other cousins.

Nigeria has a diverse culture. How I wished their eyes didn't see the color of my skin, but my intelligence, attitude, and self-control.

But honestly, I have always had a question in my mind. Is it culturally, politically, or professionally advantageous to identify as a privileged oppressed?

None of my husband's family members has ever used race as any form of identification. If you suck, regardless of your skin color, they treat you accordingly.

They have always treated my mother's family the same way they want to be treated. They consider themselves better than no one honestly.

"The collectives deny the Lord, but He loves humans." That I could say.

My husband became worried when we had our first child, his fingers shook, I could see them, even when he hid them behind him. The joy on his pale face suddenly disappeared, as he approached me at the widened hospital's labor bed.

"What's wrong babe?" I tried to get to the seed of the matter.

"I hope he... I mean I am scared he might end up like these crazy people who hate they're half white." I could feel how heavy his worries trodden him down.

# IS IT CALLED REVERSE RACISM?

# 10

I couldn't blame him, he had just become a father, and he wanted his son to be proud of him.

"There is no such a thing as white or black people babe, we don't have white or black blood running through our veins, but we have DNA from both parents," I explained to him.

Black and white are colors, not nationalities, or family but we have adapted to these titles and now they have become norms. They have destroyed our families in just mere seconds.

I never wanted to clarify this, but my black side acts like they need to be paid reparations for the actions that were made by no longer alive people. And now, the living white people should pay for what their ancestors did a hundred years ago.

You should take the bad and negative behavior and then reverse its direction, that stands as racism. I wonder if the "one drop rule" still lowkey rules our culture, and intelligence. We need to evolve past the segregation spaces we have created.

In fact, we can eliminate the phrase, "I identify as…" from now on until every single person's identity has been given equal respect.

These days mixed people prefer to identify as WHATEVER GETS THE MOST attention. So, I feel better knowing I have talked about things that worried me, oddly enough. Topics I am supposed to never talk about because of my skin color, maybe we could all possibly fix it.

Listen very carefully, most of my

mixed friends identified with whatever race with more benefits.

I have personally witnessed this, every race has privileges, but you will be surprised why most mixed people identify as black. There's more power in "a victimized side" than you could ever imagine.

You could give my black side a golden goose, and they would still talk about how oppressed they are being treated. I believe my white side tried to fix the problem.

The thing could be having the game in your hands regardless of how many times your opponents have more chances to win, which could be more precious because you can control when it will be played.

I don't like the term reverse racism; it has created loopholes for the "oppressed race" to bully and escape their actions. A spade should still be called a spade.

# 11

I am not against people identifying wherever they see fit, although the one-drop rule became outlawed in 1967. At least, I know the national mentality doesn't change easily.

I had a classmate in high school who had more black features, and his complexion aligned more with the black community. He felt more accepted and welcomed so he ended up identifying as black. Some of my colored colleagues are genuine about their identity. We all deserve to identify as we feel within our inner selves.

There must be a lot of sense if we identify according to our skin tone, but the issue here, we can never change our actual truth.

Most black people think we don't want to identify as black because it will be degrading to our white parents which is totally false. We love and respect our black side too.

They think we want to satisfy society in order to fit in, this narrative has still gone for our mixed marriages, what's wrong with marrying someone who could understand me on a personal level?

Well, the truth could be my mixed brothers and sisters who only cling to their black side enjoy the victimhood cookies available. Even when they have a single drop of black DNA, they immediately make it their own race. I love our former President of the United States Obama, but he represents the benefits of identifying as black.

I am not blaming any of us, some of us only identify as white as well because some few parents were not willing to use negro bathrooms or negro water fountains or send their children to the negro schools when there were better facilities for them.

But there have to be more benefits to identifying as black these days, you can get all kinds of government handouts, and you basically don't need to work for anything.

One thing about America, we are more concerned about identity, black people born and raised here identify as African American. In fact, it shook my Nigerian mother, the first time she heard about it.

Is it because whenever you identify with a pitied side, IT WEIGHS more?

In fact, I don't want to hear race, it should be social contrast, we are all the same regardless of our skin tone differences. The culture we get nurtured from, however, must depict our personalities.

# 12

Ignorance and racism move hand in hand, my black side must be knowing what they're trying to do because the benefits come with race-based policies, and most definitely "the victimized race" gets more financial assistance than they could ever acknowledge.

I have always wondered if my black side read the Civil Rights Act of 1964, which "prohibits discrimination based on race, color, religion, sex or national origin." I remember every American race who fought for this law. Do they even have a picture of these people?

We all know black identity comes with privileges, that money they use to pay for fake long nails and chains. We once had a neighbor's son over, he had a white mom, and his father was a biracial man, but still, he identified as a hardcore black person. Too convenient, right?

My white side keeps on doing the

work while my black side sucks on the reparations. Why don't we hear stories about biracial 's white side? They have failed to acknowledge their white families, it's like they don't exist in their world.

The racist card should work on both races, yes, you can be a racist to Caucasian folk regardless of what some "experts" claim to not be true. Our American society has the most overwhelming obsession with categorizing people into groups, and when mixed ethnicities came up, it stuffed into their theories.

I remember that European Mediterranean ancestry, their foods such as Kielbasa, red beans with rice, and curry goat, had quite a history. I sometimes wonder what race God shall call us face to face because we all bleed red.

Who has told the biracial people that their European background has no value?

The irony should be we do have white physical features, and some of us absolutely have less black DNA but still, we decide to identify with "the victimized race."

I have found myself so many times sitting my uncles down, explaining even though my skin is white, I do have black DNA, it should be the same standards on both sides.

To qualify for any state's program, you should either be black or poor, why that kind of division? It should depend on the merits and purpose of those functions.

My uncles made racist comments about my physical appearance but claimed they could never be racists because they were black. Very funny, and convenient right?

# 13

I grew up in a multicultural society, but the amount of expounded unfairness and rejection my black family subjected to me has been incomparable torture. They held me back on prejudice at every turn, they never gave me proper chances to learn my culture.

I know some of the black folks claimed the reason why we should identify as black is for affirmative action. How does that aim to increase opportunities for everyone? Very interesting.

Sorry, but I am not buying it. In a community, where black kids have gone to great success without a need for affirmative action back then.

The truth is when you drop even a single drop of ink in the water, it can never be pure. Why are we contradicting this situation? Why?

Being a victim has also been their popular tactic, and of course, a special treatment given out of guilt for the deeds of no longer alive people. The

Pledge of Allegiance should be equally served to Americans regardless of their skin tone.

Colin Kaepernick, Clay Thompson, the Ball Brothers, Patrick Mahomes, Steph Curry, Dereck Jeter, Denis Rodman's daughter, and more individuals have white mothers but still, identified as black. Most of these mentioned individuals have whiter skin than mine.

This has resulted from the black privileges, where my black folks can be rascals without facing any judgment. Do we have privileges to be discriminated against by you, as our children denounce their heritage for yours?

"We Snakes and Stars" lingo is originally Southerner American English, and also known as Ebonics.

The white Ebonics-sounding Southerner-speaking Americans still exist.

Why do black people in the USA coming from generations of LA, New York, or anywhere speak to sound Ebonics or Southerners? We have no privileges to stealing people's culture.

In the '70s and '80s, mixed kids were beaten and discriminated against by black folks because of what we represented, "togetherness." We wondered what we did to deserve such hatred.

The black folks' words were sweet in public, but the hardships they had our brothers and sisters go through, behind the scenes could make one teary.

# 14

We were the minority, we had no sides and believed in both sides. When we turned majority, still they found a way to destroy our background basis.

Why does the race card only work on the colored? No, let's have a dark-skinned person identifying as white, and we act like they're truly part of that race.

Even when black people have various skin tones from very light to dark, the African features still do show, but biracial people have both, that's a huge difference. I think we need to acknowledge our multi races and heritage.

We are equal, let's have the same opportunities without using color. Denzel Washington identifies as black, but he has never believed in racism, only in ambition, and hard work based on your dreams.

Some black people believe since there isn't any historical fact of us contributing anything to this country.

We shouldn't identify as our true selves, at least white men passed laws to earn a place in this country. Very interesting!

I understood this sort of discrimination when my son graduated from high school. I badly wanted him to attend college as soon as possible so I asked him to apply for financial assistance.

In the end, he only received three hundred fifty dollars, not even enough for the transport costs to cover his book expenses. I decided to talk to the financial advisor, as my husband and I sat down on the blue cushioned seats, in a wide entrance hall, a few black kids came.

We waited in a long line, having many students from different backgrounds. However, these black students stood out since they made louder noises of complaints about their free laptops not being Apple brand.

The disgust on their adorable faces said it all, one of the skinny girls had a free apartment, but she also complained about her cash assistance check.

Unexpectedly, I became upset and made a scene. The financial advisor quickly asked us to come to his office.

"No, they cannot be upset," I concluded as we walked into his medium-sized office.

The middle-aged man showed us how the establishment worked, having millions of dollars only funding Black minorities, such as Africans, Haitians, Somalians, and many others as long as they had black

DNA, they qualified for the funds.

# 15

The whites, Asians or Biracial people had barely any funding at all, so sad. He advised if my son enrolled as a black man, they would pay everything for him. I wondered why they based the funding on the color of the skin.

We must be proud of giving over nineteen thousand scholarships every year to people who are "underprivileged," to the point where we could barely see any white person in the crowd.

I rejected his proposal. How could I try to change my son's heritage? America, how did we end up in such a state?

# IS IT CALLED REVERSE RACISM?

IS IT CALLED REVERSE RACISM?

# IS IT CALLED REVERSE RACISM?

# IS IT CALLED REVERSE RACISM?

# IS IT CALLED REVERSE RACISM?

# ABOUT THE AUTHOR

SHARIF NSUBUGA (Author/ Writer/

Actor) is the award-winning author of "Falls Along A Lifetime" series, "The girl he left" "Polo" "Campus Tea" "Sorry, but… I'm different."

He won his first award at the Africa Industry Awards 2021, as the youngest African writer in the entire continent to demonstrate excellence in his craft, and the highest standards of ethical conduct, integrity, and civic, and social responsibility.

And his newest project, "This Master Sells Immigrant Damn Lies" The very well-known, "African Visual Rhythm" "Fool Out Of Me"

As a young creative writer, he began writing his novels at an early age, bringing out many sensational original masterpieces.

Sharif specialized in Literature Studies in English; He added

German and Russian studies. He has moved his readers with overwhelming emotions. Be prepared for the unexpected.